1001 Decorating Ideas

Apartments

Galahad Books • New York City

Contents

Introduction

At some time in our lives, most of us live in
an apartment. It can be anything from the
penthouse of a luxury high rise to a room in an old
brownstone. Some apartments have rooms
larger than in the average house, some are incredibly
cramped. Some have box-like rooms that are
all boringly alike; others have unusually
shaped ones that have lots of personality but are
a challenge to furnish.

Because of this, decorating an apartment is an art.
You have to make sure the scale of your
furniture goes with the size of the apartment, and
concentrate on playing up coordination between
its rooms. Studio apartments present a
particularly difficult design problem—multifunctional and
space-saving furnishings are needed to create an
area where you can sleep, eat, entertain, and
relax without feeling too cramped.

On the following pages are ideas for how to decorate
apartments of all different sizes and shapes.

Many thanks are given to 1001 Decorating Ideas.

Chapter 1
Studio Apartments

Creating space in a one-room apartment for sleeping, eating, lounging, and entertaining is quite a challenge. The furniture should look streamlined and be multi-functional—the sofa might have to double as a bed, the coffee table might have to be used as a storage chest as well. Built-in units can help alleviate a storage problem. Mirrors and glass-topped tables can be used to make the room appear larger. And although studio apartments seldom are large enough to accommodate room dividers, there are lots of imaginative ways to visually divide the apartment into separate areas—including using raised platforms, area rugs, and furniture set at angles.

Photos: Marianne Engberg/Design: Gail Lewis

Mirrors are used liberally in this studio apartment; one entire wall is sheathed in them, which seems to double the size of the room. The mirrored-glass dining table adds to the total reflective quality of the space. The chrome of the thin-slat Venetian blind works in conjunction with a mirrored wall below it to add yet more light and space while making a bold contemporary statement. A subtle color scheme of grays, white, and chrome is accented by a potpourri of pinks in the toss pillows, table linens, oil painting, and the long-stemmed roses. A raised, carpeted platform creates a sense of two distinct living areas, one for dining and desk work, one for sitting and sleeping. Double chaises serve as a living room during the day and as beds at night.

This apartment has an Oriental theme. Bamboo-and-cloud-patterned sheets cover the bed and walls. The sheets are a fashionable, practical, and easy way to cover the apartment's ripped and faded wallpaper. An L-shaped couch provides lots of seating and a comfortable queen-sized bed. Hiding the entryway to the apartment, and making the room seem more cozy, is a wood-framed screen of bamboo blinds. Under the window is a counter that's used as a desk top, night table, and storage area.

Photos: Darwin Davidson/Design: Douglas Sackfield

H ere, a studio apartment in a town house is infused with floral geometry that divides the living areas and unifies the space. A royal blue border-print fabric covers the sofa bed and matching love seat. Storage units built at one end of the room form an alcove, lined with the same floral print and framed with the fabric border to add architectural detail. Glass shelves in the alcove display china and accessories. Two small windows behind the couch are treated as one by constructing a lambrequin covered with the fabric border. The bold blue print also covers the chimney wall—concealing cracked plaster—and frames the mirror over the mantel. Stools, slipcovered in the same fabric, provide seating for dining at the table. Light brown paint on the walls and mantel blends prints and plaids; the same color is repeated in the draperies. The base of the glass-topped coffee table is a Regency-style luggage rack painted beige; the old straps were replaced with new ones made of sofa fabric. A Victorian wicker plant stand on casters holds flowering plants and wines.

This studio apartment was designed to give a feeling of the surf and sand. It takes its color cue from the nylon carpet. Carpeting was also applied to the front of the banquette, which provides a built-in sleeping/sitting space. Other touches are the sea-blue painted ceiling and the Formica dining counter. Ash étagères store a collection of beach glass and shells. The polyester window shade can be installed with a second layer of reflective film for extra solar protection. It provides a sleek, contemporary window covering that controls heat gain and loss. Track lights and clamp-on lamps help simulate bright sunlight. Wall-mounting the lamps adds needed reading light to the sleeping alcove. Framed photographs evoke the seaside mood.

Photo: Keith Scott Morton/Design: Allen Scruggs, ASID, & J. Douglas Myers

▼   The space-conscious occupant of this studio apartment makes room for music by incorporating a custom-designed shelf for turntable and records in a nook beside the stairs.

Photo: Fisher-HarrisonStudio/Design: Jo Tilghman

Large windows and a terrace eliminate the possibility of a closed-in feeling in this studio. The apartment is divided into separate living and sleeping areas, and the feeling of space is multiplied via mirrors, neutral background colors, and concealed storage. To avoid the inevitable monotony of living in close quarters with the same furnishings, there are different slipcovers for summer and winter. On the top left is the studio in summer colors. Plywood boxes create a separate multi-level living area for the bed, seating, and night table. Covered in a linen-like fabric, each box opens to provide generous storage. Left, the living room area in winter slipcovers opens to the tiled terrace. Ample windows, mirrors, and neutral nubby carpeting visually expand the space. Above, the sleeping area in winter slipcovers is highlighted by space-efficient track lighting.

Photos: Everette Short/Design: Barbara Brass

Photo: Photographic House/Design: Molly Siple

In this apartment with a campsite motif, the bed is hidden beneath a platform. This is done by constructing a platform and putting the mattress in a wood box with casters, so that it can roll out of sight. The brick-design floor is no-wax for easy cleanup. The tent-flap treatment of the windows, the campstools, the tent-stripe pillows, and the natural wood finishes amplify the campsite theme.

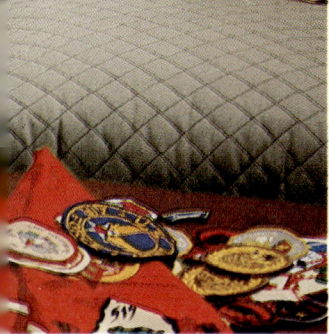

In this small studio apartment, a shortage of space is surmounted by decorating with style—Southwestern style. It starts with the sleeping/seating solution: a trundle bed that seats several and sleeps two when the bottom bed is pulled out. The sheets and bedspread, in shades of beige and brown, establish the monochromatic scheme. The walls are papered in a neutral-colored geometric pattern with an Indian motif. One wall is planked with unfinished wood and supports shelves made from wooden crates. The old trunk serves as a coffee table and also holds linens.

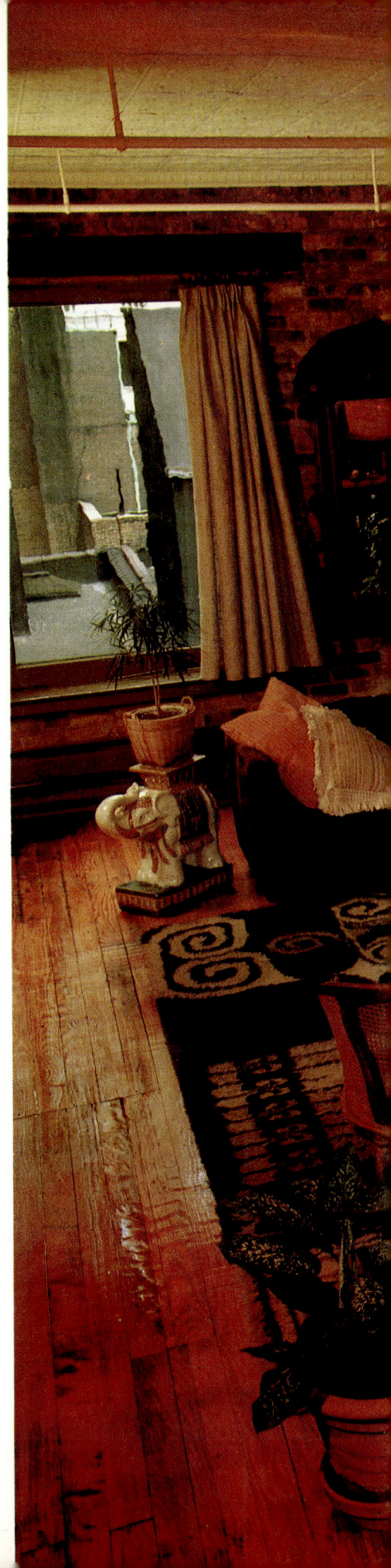

Photos: Everette Short/Design: Evan Frances, ASID

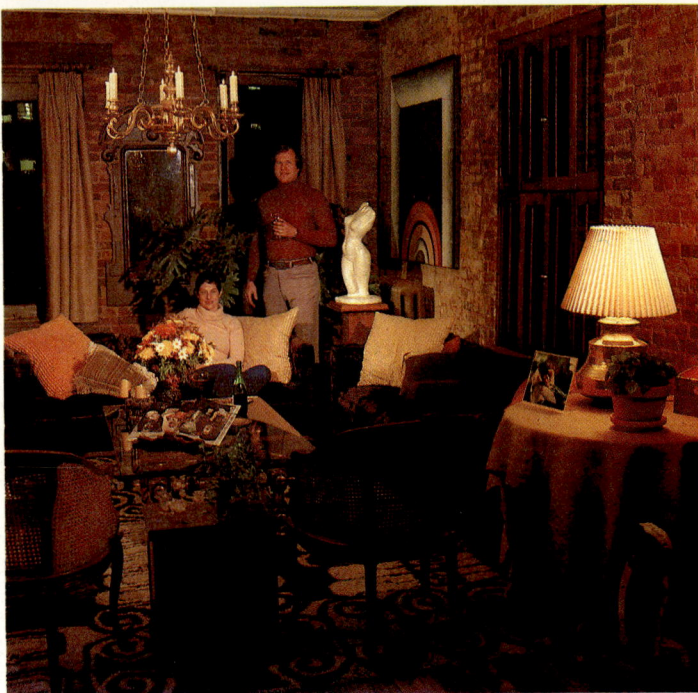

Although this loft apartment only has one room, it is much roomier than the typical studio apartment. An architectural treasure, it is built with old-fashioned attention to detail and lighted by a skylight and windows on three sides. In the living/office area, a Parsons table serves as a desk. The bedroom is raised on a carpeted platform to set it apart from the rest of the apartment. A gold curtain can be drawn for privacy.

18

An office storage wall increases the useful-
ness of this studio apartment. Four director's
chairs—which are inexpensive, comfortable, and
colorful—surround the storage-coffee table.

This studio apartment is made inviting with
neutral colors teamed with coordinated prints.
The furniture is space-saving and versatile: The
rust-colored sofa opens to provide a double bed;
floor pillows and folding chairs from the dining set
provide extra seating. There's a pine folding table
for dining and a plastic-laminated coffee table that
is great for holding snacks. The solid oak end table with white Formica top has a file drawer and
leather pulls.

A built-in armoire and a pull-down bed allow room for more furniture in this studio apartment. The room is enlarged visually with cantilevered chairs and glass-topped tables that seem to occupy less space, and with a carpet that has a geometric design and muted colors.

Photo: Hans Van Nes/Design: Shirley Regendahl

Chapter 2
Living-Dining Room Combinations

Many apartments have only one room in which to fit both living and dining areas. There are a variety of ways to divide one area from the other, while still keeping a unified design. Furniture, such as a sofa table or a modular storage unit, can be used to differentiate the living from the dining space. A subtle use of different floor or wall coverings, or a slightly raised platform in the dining area, can accomplish the same goal.

Five separate patterns are used in this appealing room and its tiny anteroom, without dizzying the head of the beholder. The secret to successfully using multiple patterns lies in choosing fabrics with ground colors that are the same hue or shades of the same hue. Here, the fabrics used all have a bright navy blue ground color. All the patterns should be kept in scale, preferably small scale. And all the fabrics should have the same colors in them. The room needs large areas of unpatterned floor, wall, and ceiling to set off the patterns and rest your eyes. The most effective background color is white, as shown in this room.

Design: Eleanor Dunlop

This room arrangement includes a versatile sofa table as a room divider behind the love seat. The coordinated dining area features comfortable chairs, an octagonal glass table, and an étagère.

25

Since the view's the thing here, the modular seating is positioned in a half circle so everyone catches a glimpse of the vista. An arc lamp offers plenty of illumination. A built-in shelf bridges the space between the twin étagères. Beneath the shelf, a tea cart on casters can be drawn up to the dining table or the seating circle with equal ease. The glass-and-chrome dining table has chairs upholstered in a terra cotta hue to echo the color of the carpet.

Photo: Fisher-Harrison Studio

A drab room like this one can be given a face-lift by stapling fabric on chairs and walls. A room divider, made by suspending fabric on tension rods, conceals the kitchen. Fabric is also hung on tension rods to cover the windows and an unsightly air conditioner.

Putty, rust, and camel—the warm accent colors of the seating area—repeat throughout this apartment as a foil to the neutral walls. A pair of chairs set diagonally subdivide the living and dining areas. Earth-tone pillows are coordinated with the upholstery and drapery.

28

Photo: Hans Van Nes/Design: Edmund Motyka, ASID

This warm, expansive living/dining area and foyer has the feeling of an adobe house. Hardboard paneling gives the walls an authentic stucco effect. The wood ceiling, created with packaged mahogany strips and wood beams, is Spanish-colonial style. Russet, self-stick, vinyl asbestos tiles give warmth to the floor. The dining area has a walnut-finish trestle table with ladder-back chairs. The banquette area has a round wicker "cocktail" table and a beechwood ladder-back chair. Plump Haitian cotton floor pillows provide extra seating. Carved wood letters and a woven wall hanging with an Indian motif flank the fireplace.

Photos: Richard Allen/Design: Sylvai Strauss, ASID

L imited space is put to good use here by placing the dining area in a small foyer and an office area in the living room. Dramatic, wide vertical stripes on the wall of the dining area "raise" the ceiling, while a long track light on the ceiling heightens the area's drama. In the living room, a print matted on burlap is hung by piano wire from the ceiling to conceal the unsightly built-in air conditioner centered on the wall above the brown velvet sofa. Vertical blinds of polished aluminum act as a room-expanding mirror or, when reversed to white plastic side, can fade into the wall. The battered legs of the glass-top coffee table are wrapped in lizard-patterned vinyl. The off-white area rug has a textured, geometric pattern. Separating the office space from the rest of the living room is a platform of dry brick (no mortar), with tar paper laid under the brick to protect the floor. A plastic-laminate desk top covers an old desk, and there's a wall-hung typewriter table nearby. A wall of shelves houses business records, plus books, television, and sound equipment. Both the wall and shelves are painted dark brown so they visually recede.

Photo: Vince Lisanti

Old and new furnishings are mixed in this living/dining room. The dining area has an oak pedestal table, bentwood chairs, and a William Morris sideboard. The living area, on the other hand, has modern seating, coffee table, and lighting. Kelly green and royal blue are the dominant colors, offset by a vivid yellow accent wall.

This apartment has a storage and display unit that flanks a desk/dining table. A light bridge across the top creates the right mood for an informal dinner for two or a full-scale buffet for ten.

A friendly but subdued elegance is achieved here by the expert use of furniture, fabrics, and background accessories. All the furnishings are reproductions except for the tripod table by the fireplace, the only antique in the room. The eye-catching rug has a Tree of Life motif symbolizing eternity, joy, and wealth. Its ruby red color gives visual warmth to the room. The Chippendale-type sofa and the chairs by the window are covered with a print simulating crewelwork. The same fabric is used for the tailored draperies and valances. The furniture is arranged so the tall clock balances the built-in shelves across the room. The wing chair is placed to allow easy access to the dining table in the bay window. Dark polished hardwood floors act as a foil for the rich rug.

Photo: Hans Van Nes/Design: Edmund Motyka

Everything in this apartment is elegant, easy to care for, and earth-toned—a combination that will make the furniture perfect for a family room if the owners ever decide to move to larger quarters. The walls are covered in Belgian linen; because linen repels dust, these walls stay fresh longer. To carry through the contemporary juxtaposition of textures, metal is made much of here. Polished aluminum blinds back up the classic arc lamp. The room's most flexible furnishing is the high and wide wall system. The oiled-walnut-finished units may be arranged in a number of ways to provide drawers, cabinets, and shelves.

Photos: Vince Lisanti/Design: Evan Frances, ASID, & Jim de Martin

Photos: Everette Short/Design: Evan Frances, ASID

The dining furniture and ceiling fixture of this living-dining room combination are in pristine contrast to the earth tones used throughout the living room area. An inexpensive, wall-hung and heat-resistant shelf substitutes handsomely for a buffet. In the living room area, tables are kept to a minimum. A table centered behind the love seat eliminates the need for two end tables to flank the love seat. And an open shelf of the storage wall plus a coffee table service the sleep sofa opposite the love seat. In the foyer, suede-upholstered benches swivel out from under their companion console table to provide auxiliary seating.

The neutral gray wall and draperies give full play to the spectacular cityscape from this living/dining room's windows. A terra cotta-toned wall warms the indoors. Dining chairs, once on the terrace, have new cushions and importance. Their see-through backs make them take up less visual space and give them an airy look that contrasts with the solid-looking wood table. A gray area rug, with tassels at each corner, is thrown over the parquet floor to separate the living from the dining area.

Photo: Randolph Graff/Design: Elizabeth Matthews

Chapter 3
Living Rooms

The living room is usually the center of activity in an apartment. Since apartment rooms often have unusual sizes and shapes—or else, as in many new buildings, are boringly alike—each one presents a different design problem. Furniture should generally be smaller in scale than that used in a house; each piece should be practical as well as attractive. In small apartments, the living room will probably have to double as a guest room and will need a sleep sofa and end/night tables.

An informal lifestyle is reflected by this eclectic mix of periods in furniture and accessories. The main decorating element is the wall covering and coordinating fabric in taupe, gray, and off-white. It's clean, crisp, and tailored, giving a toned-down backdrop to highlight the accent pieces and paintings. The wall-to-wall carpeting used throughout the apartment unifies the diverse styles and objects, creating a sense of harmony and the illusion of more space.

Photos: George Szanik/Design: Dan Weiss

This new high-rise apartment is simply furnished in a modern style, but with nostalgic early-1900's touches—banana chairs for the terrace and antique car memorabilia. The velvet seating group is composed of ottomans and two armed sofas flanking an armless model. To soften the hard-edged modern design, the chrome pieces—coffee table, consoles, étagères—have rounded edges. Patterned toss pillows on the deep blue seating units add a welcome color accent.

Photo: Hans Van Nes/Design: Ed Motyka

ere, furnishings and accessories from many nations and eras are assembled in one harmonious room. The unifying element is the color scheme—a mélange of apricot and melon hues and wood tones. Paneling of oak-grained inserts, accented by a finely detailed inlay stripe, lends the room its stately English mien. Twin area rugs subtly establish borders for two conversational groupings. In front of the window, the sofa is surrounded by étagères displaying a Chinese temple jar and other Oriental art treasures. Flanking the sofas, French bergère chairs strike the room's sole strong color note, rich forest green. Their elegant damask upholstery adds textural interest too. Against the wall, an Early American shell chest in raw pine coexists with an antique Korean wedding chest. The easy chair, the camelback sofa facing it, and the pair of ottomans compose a second conversational area. The seating is gathered companionably around a Queen Anne-style coffee table.

In this high-rise living room, printed chintz flowers vie with real flowers on the window sill. Greek key braid is on the square sofa pillows and edges the sofa hem; tassels fringe the round sofa pillows. The velvet ribbon that bands the pleated Roman shades is repeated in the hems on the chairs and ottomans.

Photo: Hans Van Nes/Design: Edmund Motyka, ASID

Photo: Marianne Engberg/Design: Gail Lewis

The visual space in this tiny apartment has been enlarged by bouncing light throughout with mirrored surfaces. Mylar-covered blinds in the living room shimmer with reflections. A mirror is used around the window to hide unsightly architectural details, and on the lower part of the sofa to "lift" and "float" it. Chippendale-style chairs act as a bridge between the modern and antique furniture.

Design: Vladimir Kagan

A sleek chrome coffee table with a floating glass top is the focal point of this contemporary living room's seating area. Lighting for the artwork is recessed into the wall behind the sofa, creating dramatic architectural details. To help maintain the feeling of space, a cabinet was custom-made to fit behind the sofa to store everything that might clutter the environment. Pure white walls let the architecture speak for itself and act as a foil for the drama of the original artwork. A pair of rust tub chairs soften the otherwise rectilinear lines of the room's furniture. The glass-top coffee table in the living room not only helps "enlarge" the small seating area but also, because it is cantilevered beyond its sleek chrome base, permits knee and foot room for anyone sitting on the sofa.

This cozy condominium has the look of a country cottage. Its small rooms are unified by their subdued, almost monochromatic color scheme. The decor incorporates plants and natural design forms. It also incorporates pattern, which appears in neutral-colored coordinates that don't overpower the small room.

Carpeting is the main design feature here—it handsomely reproduces motifs from the famous Caswell carpet now in the Metropolitan Museum of Art in New York. Crewelwork on the pillows and chair seats is derived from the carpet motifs. The shade-cloth vertical blinds and valances are an updated version of the traditional horizontal venetian blind.

This comfortable corner has a trio of
étagères, which take the place of a wall-hung arrangement so plants and pottery can be included.
Light and airy, the arrangement eliminates the
need for the window that isn't there.

In this Oriental-inspired room, a nine-inch-high sofa base has been constructed and covered with stick-on paper with the look of woven straw. The armless chairs are made by stacking two cushions on the floor; a simple metal brace slips beneath the seat cushions to support the back cushion. A cube separates the chairs, and more stick-on paper looking like straw swathes the wall behind the simulated walnut cabinet.

Photos: Stanley K. Patz

This apartment entrance illustrates the successful use of a few large objects in a small space. Access to the garden is near the conversation area, offering an extension to the room in warm weather. Built-in storage provides the space for organizing belongings. A full storage wall in the living room contains glassware, dishes, linens, stereo speakers, and other household objects. One section is used for correspondence materials and crafts, while another is an open serving area. A deeper section accommodates an upright freezer and creates an interesting enclosed entrance to the kitchen.

Photos: Charles Gross/Design: Louisa K. Cowan

Located in the southern United States, this apartment has been designed to be a cool retreat from the ever-present heat. There are a ceiling fan, shutters, and bead curtains to keep the room comfortable. And white is used lavishly, because it deflects the heat. The white lamps, a white coffee table, and white furniture look cool too. On the lighting fixture, a white ceiling fan circulates the air and stirs up a welcome breeze.

The furnishings here are lightweight and easy to assemble. The off-white frames are made of two-inch plastic that is easy to clean. Just wipe it with a damp cloth—that's all the maintenance it ever needs. The table tops of clear tempered glass are fully enclosed by the plastic frames; with no glass edges exposed, chances that you'll bump or bruise yourself on sharp edges are reduced to zero. On the love seats, armchair, and ottoman, the tweedy fabric is durable and stain-resistant. For more easy-care, there's a green indoor-outdoor carpet that looks almost like grass.

Design: Evelyn Kittay

A pair of small sofas placed face to face flank a fireplace in this living room. The long, low, upholstered kneeling bench before the hearth is a convenient perch for visiting youngsters and makes it easier on the knees to build a fire. Logs are stored inside the red lacquered Chinese wedding chest. Completing the "conservation square" are two hassocks on casters, which can be rolled whenever seating is needed in another corner of the room.

To increase floor space, the projecting mantel was removed; the fireplace, flanked by built-in bookcases, is faced with slate and wood paneling and finished with molding—a rich background for the tail of the wire peacock. Windows are covered by vertical woven blinds that are easy to open and close, let in lots of light even when drawn, yet add no visual weight to the room.

Across the room, a modified wing chair and a contemporary club chair with matching ottoman are pulled up behind and in front of a French writing table. This eclectic threesome coexists compatibly with a German clock and an African wood sculpture. Under the larger painting, the ornate antique telephone works perfectly.

Another antique in excellent condition is the small late 19th-century organ. The wall behind the organ is covered with paintings that fill the eye without filling floor space. The dark wood molding that runs all around the room emphasizes the height of the ceilings.

Multi-functional furnishings conquer the space shortage in this one-room, high-rise apartment. Because of the room's bowling alley dimensions and because of the less-than-panoramic view from the window, a large "Enchanted Forest" mural lines one wall. Pre-trimmed and pasted for do-it-yourself application, and washable for minimal maintenance, it seems to widen the room. The brown carpeting hides dirt and cuts noise from downstairs neighbors. A nubby sofa seats guests and, at night, unfolds into a queen-sized bed. On the opposite wall (not shown) is an array of inexpensive modular units to serve all storage needs, including books, records, stereo components, television, and clothing. Beyond this entertainment center, a single bed, with tailored throw and toss pillows, provides extra seating. The glass-topped desk and table take up virtually no visual space. Natural accents—the wicker rocker, shell-encrusted lamp, tweedy desk chair, and baskets—add texture to the room; pillows, posies, and earth-toned accessories add color.

Photos: Ernest Silva/Design: Patricia Hart McMillan

In decorating, a sense of style and a dash of know-how can be as good as money in the bank. No cash is needed to furnish a room like this one if you raid the attic, rescue an old baby's crib, and turn it into a settee; if you clip handsome photographs from your favorite magazine and dry mount an arrangement on gift box covers; if you scout your supermarket or farm fruitstand for an empty peach basket to use under flowerpots. The small settee—a baby's crib with one side removed—is covered with a quilted comforter. Ribbons sewn to the quilt and tied to the slats hold it securely in place. Table covers and matching window curtains, color-coordinated to the quilt, are made from striped sheets. The armoire, which dominates the room, plays a diagonally striped door against the neat squares of vinyl wallpaper. Stored within the armoire—out of sight, but within easy reach—are a television, books, bird sculptures, and a cache of baskets for every need.

By placing the sofa and love seat at right angles to each other and extending them into the center of the room, this box-like apartment without a foyer has been made more interesting. And with the strategic placement of a latticework screen behind the love seat, a foyer has been created. The screen also provides a feeling of privacy. The neatly proportioned, oak-framed seating converts, with a flip of the quilted cushions, into beds for three guests. The floor covering is a polyester fabric laminated onto a thick latex foam base. Other nice touches: Lush green and scarlet parrot print napkins are used to cover toss pillows; four small tables are combined to make a big one; painted stripes climb the window blind; and white kitchen storage bins hold magazines.

Contemporary seating pieces here are upholstered in a creamy white waffle weave knit, which shows off their trim lines. A terry beach towel with a seascape on it has been stretched and framed for the room's focal point. Its brilliant colors—electric blue, deep pink, and lime green—are used as a cue for the bright accessories around the room. Plastic coffee can lids, which have four tiny holes in each one and are wired together, serve as both a divider and wall extension.

Here is a beige and garnet living room decked in Christmas finery. Designer fabrics for the cushy pillows, coordinated wall covering on a folding screen, and a pillowed love seat work well with the painted trash-can table and the crate coffee table—one topped with Plexiglas, the other with a circle of wood. A "found" Iranian wedding certificate gets a classy face-lift with a chrome frame and bright backing to produce a spot of drama on the back wall.

Chapter 4
Dining Rooms

Many apartment dwellers are blessed with a formal dining room, but others need to use their imagination to create separate dining space. A dining room can be created in a foyer, in an alcove by a bay window—anywhere a little extra space can be eked out.

Creating storage space to compensate for almost nonexistent closets and cabinets was the top priority in designing this apartment. In the foyer turned dining room, a wall of white shutters, divided into five bays, sets up storage where once there was none. The shutters conceal an awkwardly placed window, a door to the terrace, a radiator, an air conditioner, and the core for existing electrical wiring. The window and door are treated alike with shades laminated to match the wall covering and short café curtains. It's a simple matter to un-clip the curtains and remove the Formica shelf that screens the terrace door in inclement weather. The black-and-white vinyl tile floor of the dining room continues into the kitchen.

Design: Evelyn Kittay

➤ The brown-and-white geometric motif in this small dining room is lightened and brightened by blue—blue chairs and blue accents on the airy, glass-topped table. Texture is also important here (on the candles, the fresh flowers, the tortoise ta-ble base, the rough-plastered ceiling). The open hutch, pewter accessories, and the chandelier contribute to the countrified charm.

Design: Charles Lewis, ASID, John Leigh Spath, ASID, & Ruth Brooks

In this royal red dining room, the showstopper is a room divider curtain of aluminum screening that is draped like fabric and bound with a channel-quilted cuff. Channel-quilted fabric on the wall behind the buffet and plain red fabric on the other walls echo the cuff. On the parquet flooring is a geometric-patterned area rug. Subtly lighting the scene are a ceramic lamp and crystal candelabra.

➤ To set this small dining area apart, an imported handwoven blanket was placed over the carpeting that runs through the rest of the apartment. The glass top of the hexagonal table is visually unobtrusive and, therefore, makes the area appear larger. The chairs have warm brass accents and velvety upholstery. A built-in bookcase eliminates the need for a separate piece of furniture to house collectibles.

Photo: Denes Saari/Design: Dayton's Coordinating Staff, Donal O'Donnell, ASID

72

Photo: Everette Short/Design: Evan Frances, ASID

Beautifully refinished and stained oak paneling is a mellow background for the sideboard, dining table, and chairs in this dining area. A blue-and-white Chinese rug, crystal chandelier, and "Singing Cloud" wall covering ameliorate the darkness of the wood.

This formal step-up dining alcove has a mixture of gentle curves (in the calla lily oil painting and in the tieback draperies) and straight lines (in the dining table and braid-defined chair seats and backs). An Oriental motif edges the chair hem; diagonally pinstriped ribbon makes an elegant drapery tieback.

Photo: Hans Van Nes/Design: Carleton Varney

Coordinated wall coverings play up the good features and play down the bad ones in this dining room. Unsightly pipes vanish when they're covered exactly like the wall behind them. Quilt-patterned wallpaper makes a window niche become the room's focal point and gives the room a country character.

Hot Spanish colors turn a stingy dining alcove into the dramatic focal point of this small apartment. Fiberboard is used to make the ceiling-high lambrequin, and felt is used to cover both the lambrequin and the round table.

In this Art Deco-inspired dining room, a silk-screened wall hanging is a perfect companion for the glass and chrome furnishings, and the slinky draperies. Three bold hand-painted stripes on the wall, hand-painted stripes on the lamp shade, and pinstripes in the table mats recall the stripes of the wall hanging. Accessories include a dime store mirror; shell-shaped glass dinnerware; a glass fishbowl holding flowers; and a white, spray-painted palm plant.

Color is used here to create harmony between the rooms of the apartment. Blue velvet
carpet flows from area to area, making the space
seem larger. The repeated use of the soft blue on
the moldings, baseboard, and in the accessories
is a unifying force.

A cozy eating area for two is created by the use of the same pattern on the walls, draperies, and table.

Design: Eleanor Dunlop

81

lthough the furniture in this dining room is high quality, all the accessories are from the five-and-ten. The Early American dining table, chairs, and buffet hutch have a warm country pine finish. The table expands to 60 inches with one leaf, giving plenty of room to serve eight comfortably. A blue-and-white, ribbon-striped cotton print is stapled to the upper half of the walls. A plain white cotton sheer, edged in blue ball fringe, is used for the curtains. The "rug" is stenciled onto the white-painted floor boards in a pattern that closely resembles the wall covering motif. Above the table, the do-it-yourself chandelier is a lampshade suspended on a chain in a shirred velvet sleeve.

Photo: Photographic House/Design: Shirley Regendahl

This dining area is also an art gallery. The art collection extends from the built-in shelves across the wall and appears to lower the too-high ceiling.

Photo: Darwin K. Davidson/Design: Linda Blair

A small geometric wallpaper and silvery thin slat blinds add crispness without color to this dining room. Black lacquer Queen Anne chairs combine with the glass-top dining table to create an Oriental mood. The chinoiserie bar and liquor cabinet, which helps subtly divide the dining area from the living room, also adds to the Oriental mood.

Photo: Otto Maya

Honey maple-finished furniture is used in this dining area of an old townhouse apartment. The furnishings contrast with the mini-print wallpaper, which is given more importance by being used only on a single wall. Other walls pick up the paper's background color, and trims are given a second color to add architectural interest. Left-over wall covering was used on the patchwork wall hanging, where it's combined with brown wrapping paper and colored paper accents, then mounted with glue on cardboard and an artist's stretcher. Painted window shutters are paneled in wallpaper remnants and edged with masking tape. The hutch is dressed up with shirred muslin, which is echoed on the table runner, trimmed to match the homemade, bow-tied seat pads. The seat-pad fabric also covers the wire of the chandelier that is made from a basket. Straw trivets decorate the wall above the hutch.

Chapter 5

Bedrooms

Apartment bedrooms often are quite cramped and have little closet or storage space. The furniture has to look sleek, so as not to clutter up the room, but be extremely useful. Modular storage units and platform beds are a good way to solve both space and storage problems. Color can be used to brighten up the room and to make a small space seem more important.

◄ Printed fabric appears on the bedspread and Roman shades of this apartment bedroom. The colors of the fabric are echoed in the painting over the bed. The headboard opens up for more storage space.

► Space is made the most of in this creamy camel and peach bedroom. The wall unit behind the bed provides lots of extra storage space and can be used in lieu of a night table. The mini-print wallpaper picks up the camel and peach colors.

In this African-accented apartment bedroom, sleek blond furniture is the ideal foil for the lively blue-and-brown background. The combinations of doors, drawers, and bookshelves in the modular storage units invite imaginative mixing and matching. Here, four large modules and six small ones make up a multi-functional setting for sleep, study, and entertaining. A desk is created with two 30-inch bookcases joined by a spanner; the window seat is formed from two 24-inch units; two large and four small pieces are stacked to supply the storage space on each side of the window. An African-inspired fabric wraps the room with wildlife. Shutters painted the blue of the molding and door frame are a simple window treatment for an area that already abounds with fabric. A blue area rug brightens the floor.

Photo: Hans Van Nes/Design: Shirley Regendahl

The bedroom in this loft apartment is raised to define it as a separate space. It is seven-sided, which gives it a gazebo effect. The walls of the room are covered with burlap.

Roman shades, a glamorous canopy, bedspread, and pillow furniture, all in a bold pattern, brighten this room. The sky blue of the carpet is repeated in the color used on two right-angled walls (the other two walls are white). The furniture provides storage space for an encyclopedia, a bright red television, and plants. A pair of brass lamps serve as reading lights for both the bed and the two pillow chairs. An oil reproduction of a Matisse painting is hung over the canopy fabric.

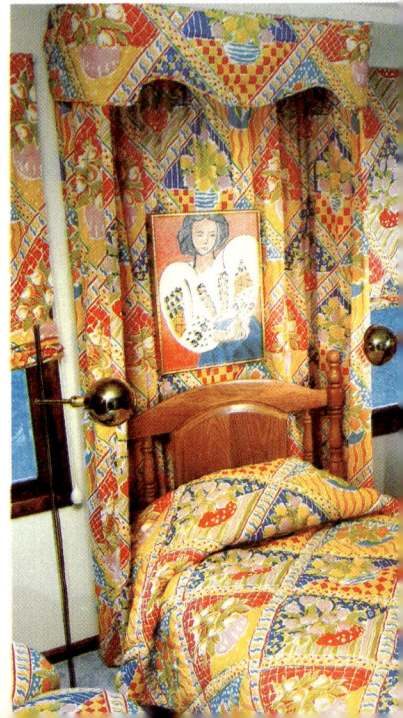

This tiny apartment bedroom is scarcely larger than a storage closet. The bed is positioned against a mirrored wall, which seems to double the size of the room. A window shade stops light—which the mirror reflects from the window on the opposite wall—from falling into the sleeper's eyes.

Photo: Marianne Engberg/Design: Gail Lewis

▼ Rich, heavy color is used successfully in this small bedroom. The three white walls, white ceiling, and white furniture prevent a closed-in feeling. The armless chair and simplified headboard give an uncluttered look.

Photos: Everette Short/Design: Evan Frances, ASID, and J. Christopher Jones

Dressed for winter, this master bedroom in a spacious modern apartment boasts a quilt of ten-inch polyester-filled puffs. Chintz and velvet squares add textural interest, as does the headboard slipcovered in corduroy. The chest at the foot of the bed is padded, with fabric stapled on. The lamp bases, which were too shiny for the soft-looking room, are muted with grass cloth. In the summer, a reversible calico quilt with matching headboard are used to give the room a brighter look.

The bedroom of this basement apartment is brightened up with silk-screened designs printed on the pillows, sheets, and night table. A wall hanging behind the bed continues the floral theme. The pillow fabric is a mixture of plaids and stripes, unified by their colors and the floral print; the same material is used on the wall hanging.